TRIUMPH HOUSE
Poetry with a Purpose

PASSAGE THROUGH TIME

Edited by

Kelly Deacon

First published in Great Britain in 1999 by
TRIUMPH HOUSE
Remus House,
Coltsfoot Drive,
Woodston,
Peterborough, PE2 9JX
Telephone (01733) 898102

HB ISBN 1 86161 563 9
SB ISBN 1 86161 568 X

FOREWORD

As we head towards a new millennium with new hopes and expectations it can be easy to overlook how significant an effect the past has had on our lives.

A passage through time offers the ultimate poetic chronicle of human disaster, development and enlightenment throughout the 20th century.

Journey into the extraordinary on a heartfelt trip through tales of past events; from the tragic sinking of the Titanic, World War Two, the fall of the Berlin Wall and much more.

The wealth of life experience and poetic talent contained within makes for a compulsive and definite poetry compilation; capturing the essence of past times and an expectant glance at how the future may unfold.

Kelly Deacon
Editor

CONTENTS

ROSWELL

It started here many years ago,
and today we still seek truth.
What happened at Roswell?
Theories still many years later,
find their way in books and on film.
Was this the breakthrough in space travel
by our neighbouring planets?
Too scared to reveal the true story,
lies and cover ups prevail.
Were they taken alive?
Were they taken at all?
We shall continue along this path,
until such time our leads run dry?
The need to know,
freedom of information,
is all we ask.
Let's not bury this historical event,
for others to find in the future.

Elaine Waite

HILLSBOROUGH SADNESS

A sporting day, a very high cost,
Ninety-six loved ones were lost,
Ninety-six candles burning bright,
As Jesus said: 'I am the way, I am the light',
Trust in Him, He bears your grief,
They are at peace, with Him is your belief,
With out stretched arms, with tender grace,
Jesus will enfold them, with loving mercy in His place.

Be not afraid, you will not walk alone,
For our Heavenly Father's promise will atone,
As each prayer is heard, by Him, and His beloved son,
His care and love, will be shown to everyone,
As into eternity, perpetual light will shine,
As in remembrance your flowers are placed on their shrine.

Irene Beynon

A WORLD WAR 2 TEENAGER

As a school leaver in '39
Just before the war began
I did not know what future might be mine
But said I'll do the best I can
War came and all ambitions
For six long years were lost
It meant forces or munitions
And for a generation youth was lost
But I met my future husband
When we were both sweet sixteen
Then as a soldier in a far off land
By him the full horror of war was seen
We were married in 1944
Ours was and is still our one true love
Our ambition is to make three score
If we get the grant from up above
The world has changed in many ways
Not always for the good
Since those precious long lost youthful days
I would have enjoyed them if I could
Young people in the world today
To you I make this plea
Don't let your freedom go astray
And *keep* your country free.

Doris Davis

THE ROCK CONCERTS OF THE CENTURY

Stored up in every star,
Thunder and lightning for hours.

Screaming skies soon rehearse
A deluge through their fans:

The sea's a concrete high-rise,
The ark's heavy metal where

Two by two most collapse,
Drowned by infernal sounds.

Marylène Walker

AMERICAN TEARS

It was a peaceful Sunday
when Japan's sun
rose among the lattice masts of battleship row
It was a Sunday
of steel and splinters
torpedoes and terror
pain and patriotism
new blood on old glory
Hickham was hell
Ewa shattered Wildcat wings
Kaneohe burning Catalinas
Uncle Sam joined another war
not much different to the others
Legend says the Arizona
still seeps oil
like American tears in 1941

Paul Wilkins

REMEMBRANCE SUNDAY 1983

Today I watched some soldiers, this being Remembrance Day,
Their memories far from happy, their medals on display.
With 'courage' and with 'bravery', they did all look the part,
Hiding what they witnessed, they kept within their heart.

They didn't shout about it, or boast how brave they'd been,
As they stood around the Cenotaph and sang 'God Save The Queen'.
I'm sure they thought about their friends they had to leave behind,
The scars, the pain, the memories, which is hoped will fade with time.

I didn't hear one voice say: 'You soldiers were so brave',
And: 'It must be sad to come round here, when some lay in their grave.'
I'm 'lucky' I've not witnessed war. 'I pray I never do'.
To fight for one man's actions seems out-dated in my view.

Why not instead, can we not find a remedy for 'peace', and stop
Those countries fighting there, where troubles fail to cease?
'Oh Father God', look down on us and help us realise,
No more those wars should be allowed: 'Through man' enough have
died.

Kathleen Yvonne Ambler

WAR

So many years before my time
Events took place that changed my life
In 1914 the war to end all wars began
A battle between man and man, changed the life of woman

Such a chain of events
At so much expense
The youth of the day
Were the ones to pay
The mud of the Somme
Swallowed more than a million
So many lives splintered, denied
Those that returned, broken in body, in pride
War between men
A continent broken
Society changed
Then war came again
In the unbroken chain
Of unresolved hatred
Women needed to help, in the war effort

When the killing was done
And men put down the gun
There was no turning back
Of societies clock
I from a generation unborn
Who did not have to mourn
Had my expectancy from life
Changed through this strife
Now at the end of the 20th century
Which churned through much misery
I can be free and live in autonomy.

S K Clark

THOUGHTS OF HISTORY IN THE MAKING

Looking back on events of the past century -
Of the unsinkable ship, sunk at sea.
The two world wars to keep our country free,
All of this gone before -
Of family and friends who fought in the Gulf War,
Blackened sky and beaches from Saddam Hussain
Of our Queen and her golden reign.

Freedom for Nelson Mandela,
And removal of the Berlin Wall,
Of presidents who took a fall,
Hope for victims of racial hate,
To the world we all relate.

Of red, blue, yellow and green,
Our preference of colour on the political scene -
All have seen better days,
Of Mrs Thatcher and her unbending ways,
At least we knew where we stood,
I'm sure she did a deal of good.

Test tube babies and sheep from clone,
What is next we bemoan!
'Why?' The millennium bug - the unknown -
Walks in space and the race for the world,
Mysteries of the 'deep' unfurled,
As the year 2,000 approaches,
My toast to the world and my country too
Is
May it bring the best for you.

Aileen Andrews

SOS TITANIC

Sunday night
the spirit of the parties high
dinner and fine wine at the restaurant
a walk upon the promenade
to the smoking room for a night-cap

Forward to my stateroom
descending the grand staircase
decked with brass and bronze
the intensity of my gaze broke
by an unpleasant tearing sound

On the bridge it's
hard to starboard!
The berg, our doom
from the lines of Robertson and Stead
futility!

A steward on his rounds
'Nothin' to worry about'
but 'tis too late
The foundering of twentieth century confidence
begun!

Lifeboats swung out,
tender moments displayed
the Strauss' an inseparable couple
Mrs and Miss Allison
much of that opinion

Lusitania and Britannic
to follow a similar fate
Technology today is impressive
but 46,800 tons of iron
is not the most powerful force on earth

Michael Bedo (14)

COURT IN DISASTER

When blaze at Hampton Court
took place
what happened to the ghosts,
elusive as the smiles
enigmatic on the portraits hung
upon walls long corridors among?
Hushed were the voices
harboured.
Did fire send spectral hosts
for sad and smoky miles?
Did theatrical occasion send
paranormal to a sudden end?
Did ectoplasm merge
with smoke,
vague theorising purge
amok?
In catastrophic scene
how did Anne Boleyn
mix aching aura then
'mongst present day firemen?
Did the ugly sin
of murder stinking through the years,
beheaded queens,
become lustrated
and lords and ladies
haunt again,
bellowed by the blistering
end to pain?

Ruth Daviat

SPHERES OF TIME

Vastness of space,
Conveys mystical tales,
Planet Mercury, Pluto, Mars,
Sun projecting warmth
Soothing everyone
Many stories have followed
The magical moon,
Masterly moving, turning
Day into night,
Controls oceans occurrence,
High water to ebb tide.
Circling our zone
Controlling rotation.

Mother Earth harmonious terrain,
Flows along charmed unperturbed,
Astronauts venture, encased amid rockets,
Launched into space, challenging
Areas unknown.
Surging forward, searching, discovering,
Voyagers, brave courageous and valuable.
Sometimes one wonders,
What would befall,
If Mother Earth in her wisdom,
Altered course,
Voyaged, her own call.

Lorna Tippett

E=MC²

I know I am.
What shall I be
When I am not?
I only hope and pray
That I shall be
That I shall see
The perfection
Of eternity.

One must have faith
In the concept
Of energy

Outwith energy nothing was
Or is
Or ever will be
When we die, as die we must,
The world we know will
Cease to be
Elementary
Nought
A picture painted just for us
The universe
Obverse
Inverse
Zero
Eternity, that never was
History, that always is
Recreated at the birth
Of each precious soul
For each human kind
An image etched within the mind
Individually
By
Destiny.

Robert Catlin

MY TITANIC

It sailed in glory with looks as perfect as man could make,
filled with their hopes, their desires and all that was beautiful.
A man's dream for the future.
But still we continue to live like that, carrying our dreams and hopes
before us, aware only of our trappings, our appearance, our search for
perfection, that we display to others; our faults and weaknesses well
hidden.

It came so silently, so huge, so unseen; until too late.
They froze, they cried, they drowned losing all their lifetimes' baggage.
Did their trappings and outer beauty help them then?
Grasping, clutching until all was quiet again.
Rich and poor became as one: Life dependant upon a space in a small
boat.

Am I like that iceberg - cold and hard, frozen through to the heart?
Do I move through life like that - damaging those around me?
Always freezing out those who come too near,
offering nothing to those who have so many needs.
Lord, touch me, melt me with your Love and your Life so that instead
of a frozen heart I may warm those near to me with your Love.
May they find warmth and Life in your Promises and know your Hope
in their dreams.

Almost another century but still we look to outer beauty.
We are still impressed by wealth and power.
Will we ever learn?
Gracious Father, I can share in your Glory, I can partake in your Riches.
I have strength in your Power.
I have no need of anything, for all that I need, I have in you.
You see only inner beauty.
The Titanic in me can rest.

Alison Horsley

BELSEN - PALM SUNDAY '98

Here is no monument of pride,
Rather a shameful thorn in a nation's past . . .
Bravely still preserved
That no one ever shall forget.
Identity photographs of young and old . . .
Groups of families and friends,
With self-conscious posed half smiles
For a journey that would take them - where?
Suitcases piled for travelling begun in hope.
Shoes that have no feet to take them on.
The bloated beasts, the perpetrators,
Indecent contrast to sexless skeletal dead.
Tattered prison stripes loosely bind
A faggot bundle made of bones.
Eyes that seem enormous
In flesh pared heads -
As if engorged by horrors they have seen.
In the cemetery row on row of mounds
Stretching to a pointed finger and a wall.
2,500 lie here, and here and there.
Two wandering people halted by a 'cleansing' crime.
Bitter stinging northern rain
Substitute for tears
Our shocked drained eyes
Seem powerless to provide.

Di Bagshawe

THE LIVING HELL

I was a soldier, serving in the First World War,
Standing in the trenches, waiting for the call!
The fear upon their faces!
Was there for all to see,
Their clothes were wet and muddy,
The stench that filled the air?
The bodies fast decaying, were lying everywhere.
Came the call, 'Over the top we went!'
Shells were falling all around.
Men falling one by one, like skittles on the ground.
The screams of the dying, and the exploding shells.
Send shivers through our body.
As we lay there on the ground,
All is silent, it's time to rest,
Before the next attack.
This living hell, when will it end?
And what is it all for?
Just for someone's power and greed.
That sends us all to war.

Florence Mary Wells

A SOLDIER'S CHOICE

Soldier, soldier, return to me
Now your babe's been born.
My heart is swimming aimlessly.
My body wretched and forlorn.

You fight for king and country
Some crazy mixed up war.
They say the army needs you
But your baby needs you more.

Marlene Parmenter

THE MASSACRES

A drum beats as she sings,
A lost love, the emptiness,
Now a scared life.
Where the children had played together,
Under a hot sun,
Amongst the green trees,
Then, living was fun.

A drum beats as they're killed,
The lost lives, the emptiness,
Forever a scared life.
Where the bodies now lie together,
Under a hot sun,
Amongst the green trees,
The living had tried to run.

A drum beats as she weeps,
Her lost life, the emptiness,
Living a scared life.
Where thousands had died together,
Under a hot sun,
Amongst the green trees,
We the living are numb.

A drum beats as she sees,
Friends' lost hopes, the emptiness,
Surviving a scared life.
Where a few now survive together,
Under a hot sun,
Amongst the green trees,
Is all their living done?

Angela Henderson

DUNKIRK DELIVERANCE

Dark manevolent smoke strokes the sea
And drifts to reveal
A mass of tiny boats, ships and thousands of men,
Smothering the beaches, the last appeal.

Waiting, expectantly to be plucked swiftly
Away from the attack.
Cold, wet, tired, blood stained glazed faces,
White knuckled clutching guns, sodden pack on back.

Smoke, thick, tears at weary sore eyes,
Tears falling, misery.
Mouths wide with despair, numb fingers clawing.
Screaming souls, agony of burden bury.

Hauled from sand to water to fishing boat,
At last to mighty ship of grey.
Again, cracking guns, choking smoke, blood and hatred enveloped
in mourning.
Cruel, absurd sick price to pay.

L Brewin

GRANDAD'S WAR

People called it the 'great war'
A war to end all wars Grandad said,
Nothing great about a war,
That leaves men maimed or dead.

Up there right at the front,
The shells around him shrilled,
From the trenches out he came,
Advance kill or be killed.

Grandad said as he advanced,
He saw many brave men fall,
Young men wounded, dying, dead,
In which no sense he saw at all.

He felt his left leg shatter,
His shoulder burn like fire,
As bullets bloodied his tunic,
He went down into the mire.

I was lucky he said I made it home,
Some lay buried where they fell,
Young lives wasted, thrown away,
As we fought in a living hell.

In dreams he saw comrades fall,
He would awake bathed in sweat,
My old one legged Grandad,
The war would not let him forget.

I hope to fight in a war,
Will never more be our fate,
Let peace reign in the new millennium,
For war my Grandad said, is anything but great.

Frederick Sowden

DEATH OF A SOLDIER

The all obliterating sound,
Swift ending of his years,
The mark was found,
Dissolving and releasing fears.

In that last outpost of mind,
Thoughts of kindred, loved and known,
Lying with his own kind,
Calcined bones in placid loam.

Under the dark uncorniced sky,
Morose dank earth
Took him in muddied mould to lie,
There to await soul's rebirth.

Idris Woodfield

BREAKING HEART

With trials and fears
Bring on many tears
It is never very clear
When one is so dear
Sickness and pain
Causes the strain
How helpless when small
Having given your all
Passing a treat
Sleeping so neat
Hoping for a smile
All standing in file
Praying in line
Things will be fine
Looking for help above
One given so much love
Swift piecing flying dart
As a breaking of a heart

Anthony Higgins

No More Steam

There's no steam trains now,
not for many a year.
Train at the buffers,
we used to thank the engine driver,
fire glow behind him,
after train ride trips
to the Southend seaside
or up to town.

Across embankments
through Essex pastures,
I remember the powerful 'Britannias'
tugging freight wagons with ease;
we waved and friendly drivers waved
to boys playing in streams.

Black engines before brown vanished coaches
passed our cricket field,
going towards London,
and I would run,
to catch the smoke in my nostrils,
savouring the oily sulphurous vapour.

The little brick engine shed soon pulled down,
the cattle siding but a memory;
the tank engines of the Tilbury line
have gone to scrap or museum yard.
We used to thank the engine driver.
No more steam! No more steam!

Malcolm Barrell

DIANA

When first on the scene you came and on the populous you gazed,
Then with intriguing qualities you left us so amazed;
Your dream of a royal marriage had come true,
You fulfilled that role so majestically - a fact we all knew;
Alas this union was not a success for thee,
It suffocated - in your words - 'cause there were three;
You struggled through post trauma to find your goal,
Fought through private pain-made time to help the less fortunate soul;
You represented our vision of genuineness and truth,
Alas taken from us while still in your youth;
In the garden of life you were as beautiful a flower e'er born,
Now in the wake of your death we are so forlorn;
God sent you on this planet to fulfil a role,
Your impact so greatly now felt - you did succeed in your goal;
May you rest in peace and now to meet our Lord,
For your great work on earth this is now your reward.

William A Ryan

CRISIS OR CURE?

Space-age life is rushing apace,
1969 moon landing;
Eagle on Tranquillity base.
Armstrong left footprints outstanding,
Fixed plaque, read with Aldrin behind,
'We came in peace for all mankind.'

John Kennedy made moon his goal.
'What can we do for man's freedom?'
Desire to be free stirs each soul,
Scope not serfdom is true wisdom.
Free and faithful dedication,
World peace from ocean to ocean.

New millennium imminent,
Apprehension when the chimes strike.
Look forward not back most pertinent,
Changes faster , be business-like.
Rights mean responsibility,
New schemes seek one fraternity.

'All Apollo's systems working'
Reported the morning paper.
The Creator's laws are coping,
On mountain tops, clouds and vapour.
Source of galaxies, strength of grace,
Help us liberate every race.

Thanks Lord for bounty and beauty,
World-wide harvests both great and small.
Hungry cry, we know our duty,
Stocks of food must be shared by all.
From greed, despair, earth seeks release,
United Nations plan just peace.

James Leonard Clough

1ST BATTALION A & S H ENTRY INTO CRATER - 1968

In a far off land across the foam,
Braw highland lads sae far frae home,
Were on parade with pipes and drums,
On the desert sands of Aden.

As a Scotsman should they proudly stood,
Their colours sure, their heads on high.
In the Garb of Old Gaul they marched and fought,
Their banners waving high in the sky.

The drum major points his mace to the sky,
The kilt it swirled, the pipes they skirled.
In proud array they marched away,
To take the Crater of Aden.

March on! March on! Colonel Mitchell cried,
As the pipers marched off side by side.
Play, play, play on, we'll march along,
And we will conquer Aden.

Now the battle's o'er, the day is done,
There's a thousand fights for peace to be won.
O'er land and sea and sky above,
May the dove of peace fly freely.

Hugh Cameron-White

ENGLAND'S DREAM SHATTERED
(FRANCE '98)

Oh David Beckham!
What have you done?
If you hadn't been sent off,
Our team would have won.

You gave us such glory
When against Colombia you scored,
By millions of supporters
You were adored.

You gave us such hope
When you scored that winning goal,
With our dreams of a World Cup,
You were England's heart and soul.

Our dreams were so sweet,
We were well on our way,
Our dreams of a final,
Until that unfortunate day.

We watched in our millions,
And look what it cost,
Our World Cup dreams shattered,
To the Argentineans we lost.

Marcus Tyler

VIETNAM MEMORIAL

Jungle grave to stone engraven
Incised in shining granite every name
Lacerated the black gash of shame
Only a touch brought tears
That it may happen again
Was in all their fears.

D Parrott

HE SAID 'YES' - AND CHANGED THE WORLD

How many statesmen, have made an earth-shattering decision?
A decision - to annihilate, an entire enemy city,
A decision - to drop the first ever *atomic bomb*.
This - was *no* decision, for a daydreaming *'Walter Mitty'*.

US President Harry S Truman - was such a man.
After the death of *Roosevelt* - he - the *Vice President* took over
the reins,
To avenge those *American* defeats - in the early war years.
This time - he would wipe off the stains.

In *May 1945* - *Nazi Germany* had surrendered.
The *Allies'* remaining enemy - were the Japanese,
Who had doggedly fought the *Americans,* for every occupied island.
It would take a bitter struggle - to bring her to her knees.

American General MacArthur planned an invasion of the Japanese
homeland
But - this invasion, could cost *one million American dead,*
He well knew - of the *Japanese 'Hara Kiri'* methods.
Yes - they would fight dearly - whilst *American* boys bled.

But now - *President Truman* possessed a new terrifying weapon,
An *atomic bomb* - the world's first - in any war.
It was ready for use - at the *President's command*
To save *American* lives - and unlock that *Japanese door.*

In *August 1945* - he said *'Yes'* - to the bombing of two cities.
In Nagasaki and Hiroshima - thousands died, or were affected by
radiation,
The effect on the *Japanese* population was catastrophic,
It signalled the end of the *war* - for the *Japanese nation.*

It took great courage - to sanction the use of this *terror bomb,*
A bomb - that would cause such devastation,
But - to the *Americans* - remembering *Pearl Harbour* and the
Death March in Bataan.
This *atomic bomb* - would be ample compensation.

Paul Gold

THE BROKEN PROMISE

Breasts heavy with milk
  She caresses her new-born
Contentedly sucking
  His first taste of life.

Capable of loving -
  Loved in return.
A bond for eternity -
  The sweet gift of life.

Violence! Disorder! Bloodshed! Slaughter!
  Ireland - Israel - Lebanon - Iraq.
Anarchy, carnage - twin monsters of war
  Crushing the breath from the not-so-long boy.

For him not the long life -
  No promise of morrows.
Caress of the graveyard -
  Cold earth now enfolds.

The sighs of the mourners -
  The cries of the loved ones.
Away tyranny, away!
  Let youth have its day.

June Hewett

INVENTIONS

We've developed cameras, mobile 'phones,
The motor car, wide screen TV,
Sonar, radar, sonic planes,
Huge metal ships that sail the sea.
We've harnessed steam power, jet propulsion,
Nuclear power, wind, waves and sun.
We've invented plastics, nylon, concrete,
Metal alloys, and the gun.
We've created complicated poisons,
And chemicals for curing ills,
Spectacles, and hearing aids,
Injections, contraceptive pills.
We've invented washers, tumble dryers,
Microwaves, cassettes, CDs,
Computers, penicillin, rockets,
The hi-fi, cooker, and deep freeze.
One hundred years have passed and we've
Developed things you won't believe.
As another century looms before us
I wonder what man can achieve.

Jan Clarke

VE DAY

I do not wish to remember
Because it makes me cry
But I have to remember
For the one who had to die.
There must be thousands of us
With a sadness in our heart
When we look back in sorrow
On the day war had to start.
They left us with a smile
And a loving kiss
The war would soon be over
We had to think like this.
Millions did not return
Way back in forty-five
Many tears were shed
For those no more alive.
We waited and we hoped
We need no VE Day
In silence we remember
As each night we pray.

E Hawkins

THEY PLAYED AND LOST

1948

Workers of the world unite,
Was the battle cry of Freedom.
Head towards the Eastern light,
To lead us out of serfdom.

This was their dream.

1960

We must work, we must build, we must fight,
We must show that Left has might.
Sacrifice is needed,
(but not by those who lead us).

This was reality.

1992

Now the dream that once drew them on,
Is on the wheel of Liberty broken;
And Soviet Russia is Russia token
As Europe East crawled to democracy.

This was their tragedy.

1993

As the workers of the world united,
In the downfall of a State so Total,
The thoughts of
Artists, thinkers, writers
Burst, bellowing through
The Walls of Silence.

And this was their consolation.

Peter Lee

ALWAYS ON MY MIND

There was no one else to compare
With his charm, good looks and jet black hair
His audience waited with spellbinding anticipation
And hearts he captivated throughout the nation
Hundreds travelled to hear him sing
Magical was Elvis the King
Loved and adored by so many
And to touch him
There simply wasn't any
A star with great magnitude
Everywhere he went being pursued
From his heart he poured out 'Suspicious Minds'
Elvis I remember
The only one of his kind
For who else could sing 'In the Getto'
With so much poignant meaning
'Love me Tender'
And I just can't help believing
It's now or never and American trilogy
The song his momma liked
Who else could sing with such great tenacity
No one but he
Sadly falling victim to wealth and fame
Until suddenly one day the Lord came
Now Elvis sings in God's heavenly choir
Amongst other great singers
Whose lives have also tragically expired
Born in Tupelo, January 8th 1935
Elvis Aron Presley
August 16th 1977 he died.

Joan Taylor

DERELICTION . . .

*(With some thoughts for those deeply affected by the
disaster at Hillsborough, Sheffield. April 15th 1989)*

So this is how it feels, my Lord,
        To be unloved and unadored,
Derided, stripped, uncovered, bare,
        And no one there to really care.
I stand, (or do I crouch?), alone.
        I hear inside one sterile moan
So desolate, stark, barren, dreary!
        I'm isolated -no one's here
To lift the burden in my mind,
        To ease the stress in all I find.
I hear no word, I see no sight
        That really helps me through this night;
This night, O Lord, that's so insane,
        So wretched, worthless, full of pain;
A pain that isn't searing, hot,
        But dulled and lifeless, like a blot
That fills my mind, my heart, my soul:
        Yet leaving but a gaping hole.
O Lord, I know that you are near!
        It doesn't stop this naked fear.
This dismal void, that forms a drain
        Covering me in grief and pain . . .

        Some covering!

Clifford C Fane

A TRUE DREAM

I saw in a mist what
looked like thick mud slipping
and children screaming, I woke
with a start, oh! dear God what
a terrible dream.
A few days later when the news
paper came, there on the front page,
the terrible news, yes, it was the
Aberfan Disaster.

Gloria A Pocock

A DAY

In the 20th century every day of every year
Had an impact on someone's life
Every day in this century
Someone, somewhere was affected by its events.
Not a day has gone by where someone
Has not either learnt a lesson, or experienced one
Or had their life turned around.
Every day a baby is born, a creature dies
A war starts, peace dies.
Every day events are turning and occurring
Moving on people's lives.
Some have a profound effect
As someone stands and fights for rights,
Others touch the world as they save a life
But most of all, throughout the world,
There are personal ones
Which open up or close a life.

D Elliott

How Dare They?

How dare they invade our space?
What's wrong with the human race?
Do they think it's some kind of a game?
Don't they have no pride, feel no shame?

They ruin furniture, crush ornaments and frames
Somehow the house never feels the same
The elderly folk are not safe anymore
So afraid to open the door

How dare they knock down old folk
Is it their way of a joke?
Put them in a desert jail, throw away the key
That would more than satisfy me

Hooligans with plenty of time
Turn to vandalism and crime
How dare they invade our space?
Society today is a total disgrace

Towards the millennium I wish to find
The crimes of the nineteenth century left behind
People can safely walk in the dark
Children not abducted from school or park

In the past doors were left open wide
No reason to fear or to hide
Children playing in the street
We're never afraid to say hello to people they meet

So as we reach towards the millennium I pray
That the government will find a way
To do away with all the crimes
And look forward to safe and happy times.

Cassie Pace

COMRADES IN ARMS

Midnight -
In World War Two in Italy.
Menacing, booming German bombers
Advancing, shedding legacies
Of death and flame:
Over the Monastery of Monte Cassino.

Below them a lone, anonymous
Grievously wounded Gunner
Who *knew* he was to die,
And shortly too.
His friend, a Bombadier, crawled out.
They lay, both dangerously exposed
Beneath Cassino's sinister shadows.
Both well aware that soon, so very soon,
The Gunner would be no more.

Bright orange 'onion' flares
Dropped by those marauding planes
Illuminated the Liri Valley
With a theatrical amber glow.

The Gunner looked into the eyes
Of his true, faithful friend.
He said, 'I knew you'd come, Jim.'
He smiled a smile both wan
And wonderful, and charged
With warmth - and ultimate truth.
Through pallid lips he spoke
Once more - 'I knew *you'd* come.'

Then quietly, so very quietly,
And undramatically,
He died.

Richard Flemington

FROM UNDER THE COVER OF A MYSTIC CLOTH
(The death of Diana, Princess of Wales)

From under the cover of a mystic cloth
The light drew the prying moth.
Thundering wings disturbed the night,
Searching with intrusive sight.
Stalking, as they ran with fear,
Their nostrils flared as startled deer
To hurtle on blind, insane,
Through a narrow neon grain.
On and on to greet the kiss,
Of death's dark welcoming abyss,
And on the wings still they beat
The moths drawn to the heat
Until, with the cool of dawn,
The world was left to mourn.

Colin Farmer

1914-18

Some went for adventure,
some went for gain,
some hoped for glory
as they boarded the train.
All went as invincibles,
safe amongst friends,
home again by Christmas
just one of the worrying trends.
No one told them of the trenches,
of gas and mud and tears,
none of them thought as they waved goodbye
that if they were lucky it'd be for years.
Underhand and then over the top
to find real guns that just wouldn't stop,
living in a hell that never ends,
surrounded by wire and bits of their friends.
Ordered by idiots, brave to the bone,
fighting over ditches a long way from home.
Killed by the thousands, more every hour,
a horror remembered by one simple flower,
a generation wasted, so much thrown away,
sold out by their own country
and the idea that war's a game to play.

M J Morris

CARNIVAL DAY 15.8.98

(Omagh, Co Tyrone, Northern Ireland)

Slugs,
Mucous Gastropods
With no shell,
Bilious brown
And green,
Chocolate box black
And blue,

Menace my delicate shoots.

Extermination
Is necessary
And
Sensible.

Salt, or pellets
Do the trick.
They liquidate,
Leaving
By the morning
A glutinous mess
And a silvery
Trail of frozen
Synovial fluid.

Perhaps I should not kill
Anymore,
But put out a
Bowl of beer.
And let them
Make their own arrangements,
And choose
Their own poison.

David (Dai) Jenkins

DEATH ROW

He is waiting
While the
World's debating
Should he live
Or die.
The electric chair
Is sitting there,
Listen to the cry
Of a mother's plea
For sanity
Now is it just
Or right,
To sign away
A troubled life
Let go without a fight.
But one must abide
By the given guide
The rules of state
To uphold.
In the end
It doesn't
Matter what others
Think for the
Punishment is told . . .
You die.

Karen Jones

A CERTAIN SPRING

As spring returns each year,
In imagination again I hear,
The bark of gun, again the scream of shell,
When our fair land seemed like hell.
Then as winter's bite lost its fury,
And new green buds grew surely.
Steel grey guns in their pits, waiting,
Gunners too, with cause for hating.
For many with dear ones bombed and lost,
Carried in their hearts the dreadful cost.
In trees, rooks were building high,
While radar scanned the sky.
See, a blip, one of ours or theirs?
From the camp a Klaxon blares,
Running feet, moving fast,
Now on target, they won't get past.
Birds were silent as guns gave tongue,
And up there, a strange bird was stung.
Metal feathers, floating down,
Good shooting, he didn't reach town.
But I still remember, tears in eye,
For someone's son who, for war, had to die.

Ruth Allerston

THE BERLIN WALL

People separated,
By a huge stone wall,
'No fairness in our rights,'
I heard someone call.

The atmosphere is low,
The sky is a raging grey,
But then the news was finalised,
The streets screaming hooray!

The scenes changed drastically,
Down low to sky high,
They couldn't wait another day,
People laughed but also cried.

And then the day came,
With millions gathered around,
The countdown with a crash,
Suddenly not a sound.

Everyone was buzzing,
Running over the crumbled wall,
East Germany had been freed,
Once and for all.

Natalie Trowell (12)

TITANIC

When you slipped into the ocean's gloom
To the cries of those for whom
In fortune's race and life's sad lottery
There was no room,
With the dowsing of your lights
Those lucky few who found favour through their birth
Scrambled into life saving rafts
And were set adrift and sent into an eerie, silent night,
Save for the lapping on the bows,
From which their guilt-ridden rescue, for all they knew,
Maybe none too soon;
But unlike those souls now free from care,
At least not altogether lost to life -
Convulsing beneath that inky waste
With nothing save a rusting metal hulk
To mark their final resting place.

And standing now in the maritime hall of ignominious fame
To whom should we apportion the blame,
This memorial to man's conceit
That thought the mighty seas to tame
And loftily proclaim himself above all natural force -
A challenge to which she ever will rise;
And to our folly and our cost
She will mockingly deliver and wreak out
Her all-powerful reply
If ever we should dain to think
That we her timeless power could defy.

John Eastaugh

1914

Nineteen hundred has come at last
and nothing's really changed
it seems our lives will ever
run on much the same
our beliefs and thoughts and ways
are firmly set in stone
we're English and we always
stand proud and alone.
Our sons will take from the land
or yet take from the mine
our daughters give us children
to preserve our ancient line
and so our bright new future
we give to our baby sons
unaware their lives will mark
the loading of the guns
for a new era comes not with
the passing of a date
but is marked by what the people
of that time will create.
Then there was an ending
of all that we had been
this century really got started
in the year nineteen-fourteen.

Helen Stamp

BALANCING THE BOOKS

I muse upon behaviour patterns of the twentieth century
As they are acted out between the back cloth and proscenium:
The hermit shelters in a shell,
Others as a parasite will choose to dwell,
Flyers high, industrious. Perchers lazy, loath to move.
Actors and their actions merge
Emulating fish, animal or bird
Or each in part,
A seriation of a vast transmorphic vista.

To some it posits evolution consummate
Others see its form in genesis defined
Uniquely, with intelligence and motivation full equipped
That millions of millennial years have now refined.

But in reality, what lies behind the achievement that I see
Projected on my mind's eye screen?
I cogitate upon the image 'Genus Homo';
This example of morphosis found a way to fly in space
Encapsulated in its own invented means
And I reflect;
There have been many negative achievements too,
One of those that we can mention is continuing perfection
Of the means to fight a war,

Need one say any more?
Yes, think of how much money we provide
For that purpose, whilst, world-wide
There are others pressing too.

I can ponder what they are,
Can you?

Gordon Padgett

MAN ON THE MOON

I was a child when man first walked
Up on the moon in the sky.
I thought it all a fairy tale
Listened and said, 'Oh my!'
I did not realise the significance
Of mankind's new impressive feat
I thought it all a fairy tale
To encourage in me dreams sweet.
I did not know Russia and
America had a space race.
I thought it all a fairy tale
As up and down Daddy paced.
I thought the stars were way up high
Put there the moon to accompany
I thought it all a fairy tale
Thought up by Daddy to amuse me.
How little I knew of the man on the moon
And the significance it held;
I thought it all a fairy tale
As my daddy my hand held.
Now I know it isn't a tale,
I know now it is a fact hard
But I liked it as a fairy tale;
I never liked facts too hard.

J E Alban

THOUGHTS OF DIANA

Lying in my bed with my radio on
Slowly drifting to sleep after the day had gone
I suddenly woke when the news was read
Princess Di's had an accident, we think she is dead.

I couldn't believe this news I had heard
For a moment or two I couldn't say a word
I woke up my husband asleep in our bed
And told him the news, Princess Di is dead.

At last I finally drifted off to sleep
To wake that morning and hear the newscaster weep
As he told the story of the way she died
I realised then - they hadn't lied.

With such a lot to live for Di should meet her end
In that underpass in Paris with Dodi, her friend
They loved each other, it was clear to see
From the newspaper articles and on the TV.

Those next few days before the funeral started
Everyone was sad that she had departed
We remember the day she and Charles got married
And the birth of William and then Harry.

Every newspaper cover, and news on TV
Di was the subject for all to see
Showing tours she had done and her latest fashion
And the work done for charity which was her passion.

On the day Di was buried the nation mourned
A two minute silence as the carriage was drawn
Strong words were spoken by her brother Earl Spencer
A carpet of flowers showed, we failed to protect her
Thousand paid their respects and heard Elton John play
Candle In The Wind which he sang that day.

F Baker

WAVES OF TIME (SCOTTISH CLEARANCES)

His head is in the clouds, his back is to the land,
He frowns upon the sea, and the ancient fisherman.
His fine clad feed held high, upon the mortared stone,
Not an inch of Scottish soil does spoil his lofty throne.
A statue on the Ben, a monument so still
The heart is cold, the eyes don't see,
The ears are deaf as well.
Why change the throne of this dark knight,
which points to deeds he has done?
When there are people here and people now,
and children yet to come.

From the Ben we can see, the view so far and wide,
and day by day, new hope can rise,
and wash o'er this land to refresh
just like the turning tide.

His greed for wealth, his use of power,
he has done what he has done.
But are these evils seen in him, to only him belong?
So, lift your Scottish head up high
and look for the truth alone.
And in search of that we will become
an extraordinary nation.
Our Celtic past our Scottish future, surely they mean more,
Than a sad old man, whose vanity
sought an effigy to watch our shore?
With all his wealth and all his power what of him became?
As like the earthly lives of all of us . . .
the dirt from whence we came.

Alpason

20TH CENTURY MEMORIES

The millennium is approaching
The twentieth century almost gone;
Out of all the passing centuries
This has been a memorable one.

It's had disasters like the Titanic
And World War One and Two;
Assassinations of great men
Like Kennedy and John Lennon too.

There have been many inventions
Too numerous to name;
But here are just a few of them
I'll mention all the same.

The motor cars and aeroplanes
That help us get around;
Computers, TVs and videos
All electrical things are found.

And then communications
By fax and telephone;
Just take a look around you
At all the goods you own.

Vast improvements made in medicine
Cures that could not be found too soon;
And wonders of the space age
With men walking on the moon.

So as the millennium approaches
One wonders what we'll see;
After such a memorable century
As this one has proved to be.

Ann Forshaw

THE VEIL

The veil of uncertainty fell over America.
A president struggles with adversity.
Greed and hate surround him
As we stand back and view him with compassion.

The veil of despair fell over Ireland.
The bereaved are swamped in their grief.
The pain and the evil affects everyone
As they struggle for ease and relief.

Lord, stand by them in their anguish.
Help them to bear their sorrow.
Lord, have pity on all sinners
And lift the veil of agony on each tomorrow.

Mena H A Faulkner

TOO HARD

Am I trying too hard
Should I go with the flow
Would it really be that hard
To give it a go
To choose a new path so late on in life
Seems such an impossible task
To let it all fall
Seems to be what's in store
If I don't keep it together
But to find the direction
And break out of the protection
I have built around me
I come out and visit but it's never enough
With the millennium approaching
I'll need more than coaxing
To step out and ring in the changes
But now I have words free flowing from pens
To combat the fear to befriend
The year 2000 maybe it's not that scary
Am I trying too hard should I go with the flow
Would it really be so hard to give it a go.

Alexander Robertson

JOHN F KENNEDY - THE LEGEND

1963 the end of a great man
John F Kennedy US President
What a man, what a legend
This legend lives on in the hearts of millions
His assassination in 1963
Was a loss to the USA and the world
He was a great president
And would have been better
Well this awful day, 22nd November 1963
In Dallas Texas USA
John F Kennedy shot by a gunman
Lee Harvey Oswald was cast for the shooting
He too then was later shot by Jack Ruby
Well the John F Kennedy legend lives on
Memories all over the world
One in my home city of Birmingham for one
The great man, great leader and a great president
One of the disasters of the 20th century
A true loss to all
The legend lives on in our hearts
John F Kennedy.

Michelle Knight

WORLD WAR 2

I was born in 1930, so I was nine when war broke out.
When the first sirens went, I was alarmed without a doubt.
Mother rushed out in the garden, with an enamel mixing bowl,
Told me not to go out, I was just going for a stroll.

Churchill spoke on the radio, we must dig for victory.
If you don't grow your own food, there will be none coming by sea.
The bombs were very frequent, they dropped them every night.
One of the incendiary bombs fell, the house was nearly alight.

Out came the stirrup pump, lots of buckets of water.
I helped put it out, Dad said I was a good daughter.
We were short on food, we were given ration books.
Mother made meals out of next to nothing, they had to be good cooks.

We had to go to lessons on first-aid every week.
They used me as their victim, I thought that was a cheek.
I was swathed in bandages from foot to head.
If I had been really hurt, by the time they'd finished
                                    I would've been dead.

Clothes too were on the ration cards.
Growing up, I found it hard.
No fashions like they have today.
It was mind that dress, if you go out to play.

At night, the bed had been put on railway sleepers.
Under it was put a mattress, so we could close our peepers.
It was hard on the floor, we had to mind the lights.
Black out was compulsory, it was black as ink at nights.

But I lived through that terrible time.
Just over the bridge they dropped a land mine
Rutherwick Close was flattened from one end to the other.
People were killed, mothers, sisters and brothers.

At last war came to an end.
We celebrated with all of our friends.
We were all very close, during the war.
You were welcomed in anyone's front door.

Sylvia M Harbert

THE OMEN

(A poem about the Titanic)

Barring the turnpikes of the sea
She staggers the motion of the waves,
Cursing the dreams of eternity
Whose billows hold her bellows slaves.

Maidenly glided the steel through the deep,
Maiden the voyage the barnacles ride;
Woodworms will waken the dead from their sleep,
Turn back the indifferent folds of the tide.

Dazzling, the ornaments decking the halls,
Gay is the pattern of feet on the floors,
Bright is the red of the blood on the walls
And frantic the hammering on the locked doors.

One day the rich will hold out begging hands
And walk on the decks where their last hours were spent
Before the sand swords and the saltwater strands
Slice through the silence and make them repent.

Where's the reminder? In pitiful state
Down on the seabed she cries out 'Retreat!'
Taunts those who tempted the cruel twist of fate;
Who dare to think well of the Titanic fleet.

Sarah Levene (13)

'WE SHALL OVERCOME'
(dedicated to the memory of Martin Luther King)

'We shall overcome - one day,
- let my people go'
I heard you say,
before they shot you
on that fateful day.

'We will all be free - one day,'
your faith moved you on,
onwards to victory -
hollow sounding now
in the light of this new day.

Black and white together -
a recurring dream of yours,
now gone, over,
down the pan -
brutally murdered before it began.

Killed off the vision -
beaten up the remnants
till they died -
broken in spirit,
twisted inside.

Only through music
do they survive -
live on,
have not yet gone.

Maybe,
one fine day,
the vision
will return.

Maggie Smith

WAR

A million miles away,
A war is in full swing;
But here from day to day,
It doesn't change a thing.
I can still buy the petrol,
And drive down into town;
And buy the dress I'm dreaming of,
In shades of green and brown.
Each morning I switch on the news,
And a few more lives have gone,
Powerful men won't change their views,
And still the war goes on.
A few more wives are widows,
Gone, one more mother's son.
But still the armies battle on,
'Til one can say; 'We've won.'
But what happens when the war *is* won,
And people's lives left shattered,
Who's going to pick up all the bits,
Who's going to say 'It mattered'?

Suzi Vanderborght

WHY?

As you fall to the ground I wonder why,
Why you don't scream out in pain and agony,
Is it because you don't have the strength to go on,
Or is it because you've had enough of the deadly sirens?
Why did it happen to you?

There's bombing going on all around you,
But I don't suppose you can hear - can you?
You've closed off from the world now,
You're on your own - with no-one to guide you.
Why did it happen to you?

What will your family do? What will they say?
When the dreaded telegram arrives they will crumble,
Not knowing what really went on.
Cursing that damn German leader - Hitler.
Why did it happen to you?

Your lifeless, bony body just lies there,
Waiting to be buried in the cold, dark, slippery soil.
I watch you sink slowly down into it.
The further you go down the less I see your body.
Why did it happen to you?

I watch as men run from trench to trench,
Taking your place on the front line.
Some half asleep from patrolling no-man's-land,
Others sighing as they trudge on tired, hungry and exhausted.
Why did it happen to you?

We will never forget you,
You will always live on.
Our hearts miss you every day,
But here's one question just before you go,
Why did it happen to you?

Grace Sutcliffe (14)

HUMAN MINDS - HOLOCAUST

Human slaughterhouses,
Blood-bath of Jews,
Built by humans,
And thought up by human minds,
Black hearted and disturbed human minds,
Of monsters that didn't care.
Human hands built Auschwitz and Belsen,
Ordered by evil human minds.
Camps of terror, death camps that
Didn't care about life.
Camps where evil minds enemies were dealt with,
Through shooting, work and gas chambers
Disguised as showers.
Millions of men, children and women,
Young and old,
Murdered under the evil claw of the Nazis.
Men with evil minds were in the end,
Killed themselves,
By courts of law,
But the men who performed these massacres,
Still walk this planet,
And soon will die.
Evil,
With evil minds.

Rob Tuffnell

THE RED BERETS

They came so bravely
From the sky,
Now in their
Grave they lie.

The silken parachute
Is now their shroud,
With which they dropped
Out of the cloud.

The Red Berets are heroes
Was our cry,
We had not thought
To see so many die.

Arnhem and Airborne
Are now as one word;
Our freedom so dearly bought,
One great tear
The sword hath wrought.

With pride and thanks
The Nederlands remember,
Forever
The days they fought the tanks.

Peter McCreary

THE KING

He was born in 1935
in a Mississippi town,
No one could have known back then
how he'd turn our lives around.

He won the hearts of many
for he sang right from his soul;
all the people named him
the King of Rock and Roll,

But then the world fell silent
whole nations stopped and cried,
And I watched it on the TV
the day Elvis Presley died.

But don't you worry Elvis
for we all know who you are,
Shining brightly in our hearts
you're still the biggest *star.*

Lynn Catherine Noblett

CHRONICLES OF THE 20TH CENTURY
(Dedicated to Afifa and Fahad)

I remember, I recollect the day
when it was announced, the day in television
that at such time man is going to land on the moon
I did not believe it.
It is mere propaganda to deceive the mass
as so many uncertainties were involved
in such a project.

I and fellow youth were stuck to the television
anxiously waiting the moment
on that day, on that night
showing man is landing on the moon
in front of you
in fact actually right in front of your very eyes
direct - not in secrecy, hidden.

I have travelled so many times by air,
still I would not like to travel to the moon.
Maybe I am a cowardly person
that is why I wonder and wander
what will happen to the person
if anything goes wrong
as I do not want to die
so miserably so distressingly
hanging, circling round, encircling earth.
In spite of all this
this is an outstanding work
keep on doing it, exploring, acquiring knowledge
which is the nature of humanity
life-blood of humanity.

Ghazanfer Eqbal

THANKS FOR PEACE

The church stands quietly
Surveying the scene,
With memories so clear
Of all that has been.

Down through the years
It's seen conflict and war,
Then the bells told the world
That there was peace once more.

The people came in
To give thanks for the news,
Quietly, with hushed voices
They filled all the pews.

They prayed and then sang
With wonderful praise,
Thanking the Lord
For His wondrous ways.

Julie Brown

ATLANTIC CONVOY (JANUARY 1943)

Mist swirling waters, a grim grey dawn:
There all around the ocean rose and fell
To the horizon - as far as eyes could see,
And the heaving convoy kept us company.

A line of ships steaming 'fore and aft'
With others stretched to starboard and to port.
So in their midst we found protection then,
A ship carrying almost two thousand men.

Ships of less import guarded our flanks,
Whilst those oil laden, troop laden, sailed between,
Like a flock of sheep we were driven on -
Our dogs, the pitching corvettes on the beam.

In a wide conflict a minor part we played
                    on our journey across the sea,
Sailing onward to some distant destination
Each one then wondered what his fate might be.

Jack Judd

RMS TITANIC
(in memory of the passengers and crew)

You kept your location secret for more than seventy years,
Your fate broke the hearts of thousands of folk,
And still moves the world to tears.

Your New World seeking passengers cheered and waved
When you sailed from Southampton's shore,
Oblivious to the hidden danger that was to lie in store.

From the midst of the frowning Atlantic,
An iceberg drifted into view,
Alas, Titanic's destiny was inevitable,
There was nothing the captain or crew could do.

Fifteen hundred people perished on that cold April night,
As the luxury liner heaved for the last time,
And then submerged out of sight.

Sandra Edwards

MY HOPE

Let countries start afresh in the year 2000,
How often moneys have been badly used,
The people crying out for food,
There is no hope.
But there is hope.
People in neighbouring countries waking up,
Moved to pester their governments to
Cancel debt.
Hope flowing back in to countries bereft
God is with them.

Jennifer Barrow

THE DUNBLANE TRAGEDY

The whole world was touched with such sadness
On that ghastly day in Dunblane
Those innocent children just shot down like that
By a monster that didn't know pain
Mothers waved their goodbyes
As they ran into school
Not knowing the horror ahead
For within a few hours
The whole world had news
That those children had all been shot dead
Tragedies like this
Make our blood run cold
But what else can we do but pray
To pray for those families with so much to bear
With the shock of that horrible day

Euphemia McKillop

TWO GERMAN PILOTS, 1941

It was 1941 when the bombers they did come
A bomb and a land mine fell from above
The bomb landed in the Luggie, the river nearby
But the land mine hit a field near Torrance
Blew everything sky high
The people living near fled for their lives
Some others just screamed and tried to hide
We heard the bangs and to the sky gazed
And saw a plane coming straight for our place
We had no time to even run
For all of a sudden there was a bang of a distant artillery gun
Its shell hit the plane threw it high in the sky

As the plane blew up its crew were to die
Next day we found the crew on the hilltop high
They were two very young lads, still not grown men
Far too young to die on our Scottish glen
We took those lads and laid them to rest
Two German lads who were put to the test
By a man called Hitler whose greed was great
A man the world learned to hate
Yes was 1941 when that plane came down
And buried two brave lads deep in the ground,
Today I could go to the play where they lay
At the foot of the Campsie glen
Where there as a child I once laid flowers
On the graves of two very young men.

Maureen Smith

KRISTALLNACHT MONODY

*(For the thousands who died, were injured, or arrested on
9 November 1938)*

It was the worst of times
Nothing would be the same again
Those mindless bully boys are feared still.

It was the worst of times
The seven score or more
Who died that day or night
Reach out to us in time

A testament of Courage,
Hope, Truth and Love
Was sacrificed for us that November night
In nineteen thirty-eight.

It was the worst of times
Nothing would be the same again
A New Age dawned that Night.

Richard Stoker

THE GIANT LEAP

Throughout our history the moon
Has influenced mankind,
And long ago was said, at times,
To disarrange the mind.
Folklore once suggested that
The moon was made of cheese,
And in the children's nursery rhyme
A cow jumps it with ease.

It has remained a mystery
Up there in outer space.
Denied its hidden darker side
We only see its face.
Noyes's 'Ghostly Galleon'
Describes it perfectly,
The so-called Hunter of the Clouds,
Stalking stealthily.
'Distance lends enchantment,' when
Thomas Campbell wrote,
He might have had the moon in mind,
So distant and remote.

Unchanging and inviolate
Since the world began,
And, till this very century,
Beyond the grasp of man.
Suddenly all that has changed,
(Who'd have thought so soon?)
One day, in nineteen sixty-nine,
A man walked on the moon.

Frank Jensen

THE FIGHT FOR COAL

In forty-seven the Government, they nationalised our coal
With machinery they did advance toward their ultimate goal
And just as Dr Beeching, the railways did axe
Lord Robens was appointed, the miners for to tax.
Then throughout the sixties those miners heard the call
If you accept a small rise now, we'll not close pits at all.
Technology was improving at an alarming rate
But not one of those poor miners could possibly foresee their fate.
The work force it diminished, small pits were closed down
And Bevin Boys with helmets on were no longer seen around.
Then a man named Scargill appeared upon the scene
To rally all the miners, be united, was his scream
And unite the miners did in nineteen seventy-two
They really showed the Government what Union strength could do
For seven long weeks they battled, flying pickets to each yard
To move any coal from place to place, they made extremely hard
Now Edward Heath had Wilberforce to check the miners' claim
To show it was unfounded, that was Ted Heath's aim.
But Wilberforce, to his surprise, he proved the miners right
He said, 'Give them their money, they've surely won this fight.'
Now we've moved into the eighties, Thatcher's at the Tory helm
Unemployment's rife throughout the land, there's sadness in the realm.
The steelworks have been savaged with governmental cuts,
McGregor was fetched from the States to crack a few hard nuts.
With the miners now his target the writing's on the wall
If McGregor gets his way, there'll be no pits at all
Redundancies have started for those over fifty-five
The experienced are leaving, there will be no pit left alive.
Now we're in the nineties and the few pits that are left
Are once again in private hands at a price that was sheer theft.

Allan Young

ENTREATY

Our fathers stood and talked and lied
about national duty and national pride
nowhere to run and nowhere to hide
and here they stand at a son's graveside.

Go to war and save some face
fighting, surviving, in a harrowing place
longing to feel a loved one's embrace
where is my God, and where is his grace?

Diseased, muddied, injured and chill
their air around here will never be still
there may be a way but I've lost my will
of king and country I've had my fill.

The crosses stand, row upon row
in fields where blood-red poppies grow
the route to peace is long and slow
when we reach it, please let me know.

Nikky Braithwaite

DON'T LET THEM BURN THE BOOKS AGAIN

In nineteen-hundred and thirty-three
In that far land called Germany
Nazi Adolf Hitler came to power;
Then dawned history's darkest hour.
He was nothing but an empty shell,
Possessed by a demon straight from hell,
Who swayed millions with his oration
How he was to save the German Nation
Then he bid his brutal Nazi hand
To begin their butchery throughout the land -
Books were burned, shops were shattered,
Anti-Semitism was all that mattered.
In nineteen-hundred and thirty-nine
Hitler invaded Poland, crossed the line,
Waged war with England and the world.
The wave of suffering was unfurled.
Amidst the sights and sound of battle
Jews were herded into trucks like cattle,
Little knowing that their destination
Was the hell camps for extermination.
Auschwitz, Belsen and Buchenwald:
Their horror makes the blood run cold.
Starved, tortured, gassed with Zyklon B -
Jews died in showers in agony.
Men, women and children, none were spared
Some shot and beaten, no-one cared.
The chimneys of their crude crematorium
Belched black smoke, but not in memoriam.
Some thrown into mass graves of lime -
Some still alive, how long a time
Until the bulldozers covered them in?
As if anything could cover this sin
Of massive and monstrous genocide
Which some have tried so hard to hide!
It is not enough to grieve and regret.
The world must not be allowed to forget

How maniacs made mad with power
Sent millions to their final hour.
Let their sad memory forever remain
To ensure it can never happen again.
Don't let the dead cry out in vain;
Don't let them burn the books again;
For in books the records are set
To remind us all, lest we forget.

Sheila Whitehead

DIANA - THE PEOPLE'S PRINCESS

I still remember that very day,
When I was in my bed,
Lying awake, listening to my sister say,
'Diana is now dead.'

> At first I thought she was lying,
> But I soon knew it was true.
> I can still hear my mum crying,
> Just as I was doing too.

Diana's death was very tragic,
She was ever so unique.
Over the world she spread some magic,
Helping people is all she *seeked.*

> Her funeral was held on Saturday,
> She touched the nation's heart.
> Althorp Park is where she now lies,
> Of the heavens she is now a part.

Fahmida Aziz Qureshi (11)

31ST OCTOBER 1984
(A tribute to Indira Gandhi)

Eight bullets in a feminine frame;
Oh, the sights I see are vile, weirdly.
Death in Fight-for-Freedom's name.
What a gentle, smiling, trusting lady!

The scene is the shrine of Indus valley
Civilisation where old river of history runs.
They claim they'd won her with the volley
Of two trained and treacherous guns.

That cowardly murder, blatant sin,
Is being celebrated with festivity
By the killers' acclaimed kith and kin -
Here, in England. Whither dignity!

Man has matured, we proudly deem,
In our humankind's recent history.
But insufficiently, does it not seem,
To live in love and harmony?

Kopan Mahadeva

DIANA

A shy English special rose
blossomed for the nation to see.
Such love and warmth to radiate
bringing much joy and harmony.

Such compassion deep within
great this courage for all to share.
Those kindly words and sunny smile
the gentle touch, that unique flair.

Reaching out where're she go
devotion and such tender care.
Calming those fears and hopes renew
spreading happiness everywhere.

All seeds planted soon to grow
people united now as one.
Your spirit lives eternally
a hug, laughter, beauty, much fun.

In our hearts for evermore
this glittering light always glows.
In peace at rest, though watching o'er
a sparkling star now gently flows.

Margaret Jackson

THE ATOM BOMB

The bomb was aimed,
It dropped, exploded,
Shattered existing structures,
Debris flew in all directions,
Overwhelming noise deafened,
For seconds the world was in turmoil.
Then the tumult decreased,
The dust settled, silence fell,
No familiar landmark stood,
The devastation complete.

Standing at its centre
The figure of a child,
Frightened eyes open wide,
Seeking that security
Of familiar faces she once knew;
Men with cold and staring eyes
As vacant and expressionless as her own,
Lives shattered for a generation.

Rita Hardiman

THE SINKING OF TITANIC

Titanic was the biggest and most desirable ship there was,
It was also a boat of beauty,
Which now lay's at the bottom of the Atlantic Ocean,
Surrounded by nothing but water and fish.

Titanic was sailing for the first time across the North Atlantic Ocean,
The captain was aware that there had been sightings of icebergs,
But he stood there and ordered more speed,
It was an iceberg that brought Titanic to its doom.

The great ship Titanic will always be remembered,
From its first and last voyage,
From all the deaths that took place,
And from all the souls that rest deep in the North Atlantic.

Lynsay Brockhill (14)

GHOSTS OF THE TITANIC

As we raised up the old Titanic
From the mighty deep dark coasts
What of its mysteries
Did we too, dig up the ghosts.

Are they haunting the *old murderess*
Would this be their revenge-quencher
All wishing to speak
Of their fatal adventure.

We wonder on *what* they would tell us
Those deeply unfortunates
Would it all be of
Happenings in their last minutes.

The day the mighty iceberg was struck
By *'unsinkable'* Titanic
Most were hysterical
Some bravely kept up the music.

Those ghosts must surely travel, so lost
Moaning for their sad losses
Does the sea care at all
In her splashings and tossings?

> Oh rock-hard iceberg
> What have you done -
> But sorted the survivor
> From the sea-claimed one.

Barbara Sherlow

A LOOK BACK

Over the past 100 years,
there have been times
when people have feared and cheered.
Great people were born who created inventions,
for the very best intentions.

The years have seen the human race
evolve to a greater place,
where people can chat to others on the PC.
That wasn't even thought of in the year BC!

People say, the end of the world is nigh,
but they've been saying that since
I was knee-high.
Let's hope this century sees more happiness
where children starving no longer happens.

We can make a difference and change.
As we hold the destiny in our hands
we decide where we go.
So let's end up in a place,
where we would all love to know.

Cheryl Rock

JOHN F KENNEDY

A special man was killed that day,
young and in his prime.
His love of life and country
was to be his only crime.
He wanted to put the world
to rights in 1963 by stopping all
the fighting that there would surely be.
But money talks and wars pay well
think of all the arms to sell.
No matter who died, no matter who fell.
Now the story is too big to tell.
So the men who did this will never
get caught, because men, like weapons
are easily bought.

Sandra H Seed

A NIGHT IN 1940

'Twas a clear moonlit night in September 1940
When my eyes sought various shapes from my window
Blackout curtains pulled back in the darkness of the room
Then sirens blaring out a crescendo.

The noise of throbbing engines broke the stillness
The invaders had started their nightly alarms
Down to the air raid shelter we scampered
With a baby nestling in my arms.

The shelter constructed out of bricks and earth
Was the best thing we could do
In a garden we loved so much
Where doves would bill and coo!

Then humming, drumming overhead
Followed up by terrific bangs
Our enemies were giving us all they had
And a bomb dropped in a bin of cans.

The windows smashed, the TV was hurled
Halfway through the massive space
Across the road we heard the screams
Of someone in terror and out of place.

The morning came, my baby cried
Covered in dirt and dust
When we emerged we saw the chaos
To go across the road we must.

People were standing, staring, shocked
The house was rubble, I looked with dread
Two old people living happily together
But now their bodies lay there - dead.

We went back home and wept with grief
For those who had lost so much
We prayed for peace in all the world
For love, understanding and God their hearts to touch.

Eileen Chamberlain

BORN TO BE KING
(Prince William Arthur Philip Louis - 21st June 1982)

O little boy of Royal birth
  Stepping into a world of strife;
Bringing that beautiful innocence
  That dares to challenge this war-torn life.

You tumbled through stars in a troubled sky
  Bringing laughter and love to this Isle;
To show us just how we have missed the way
  With twinkling eyes and dimpled smile.

So welcome you were little King-to-be
  And recalling from far-off ages too
That a Star shone brightly for all to see
  How we hoped to begin life anew with you.

So keep your chin up high, my lad
  'Twill be easier than it would seem
For we'll stand behind you man to man
  O king of our future dream.

Margaret Marsh

ELVIS

They say that Elvis was the King
But others around could also sing
Peggy Sue, she made us jive
And Bill Haley made us feel alive.
Cliff's Living Doll was the cream of the crop
And took his record to the top.
Heartbreak Hotel was a very sad place
So we sang Amazing Grace.
If he mended his wooden heart
Paul and Paula would not be apart.
The Beach Boys made the girls all swoon
But we made do with Annie's tune.
With his music, which was quite a thing
Yes, I would say Elvis was the King.

Colin Allsop

HIS WAY

(A tribute to Frank Sinatra)

Born in Hoboken the wrong side of the track,
he rose to lead the 'Hollywood pack'.
He was the 'guvnor' - chairman of the board,
a star that millions did applaud.
He started as a bar room singer,
he became the greatest big band swinger.
Millions enjoyed his vocal skills,
his lyrical magic giving many thrills.
The voice of the century - singer supreme,
his songs enhanced many a romantic dream.
An actor powerful, magnificent, sometimes mean,
a giant indeed of the silver screen.
Small in stature, a giant on screen or stage,
Magnificent, proud, a fitting adage.
That commanding glance from his piercing eyes,
as azure blue as California skies.
His wondrous voice, his dazzling smile,
An icon with charisma, panache and style.
A friend of stars, presidents, princesses and kings,
now he has left us on angels' wings.
Forever a warm memory we will retain,
Now at comfort in Paradise he will remain.
His songs and films with us forever and a day,
'From Here to Eternity' he did it 'His Way'.

Reg Summerfield

FAREWELL, OUR QUEEN OF HEARTS
(On the death of Princess Diana, 1997)

No more for her,
The electrifying flash of the camera bulb,
The paparazzi pressing her on every side;
The financial race to snap a touch or kiss,
In such suffocating pressure she died!

No more for her,
The criticism of each loving, thoughtful act,
The touch with ungloved hand, the hug,
The censure of an overwhelming compassion,
The disapproval of an establishment, so smug.

No more for her,
The sheer sense of fun of a caring mother,
The woman's frantic search for another's love,
The gentle sharing in worldwide horrors,
These now exchanged for sudden rest above.

No more for us,
The warm smile of a beautiful princess,
The national pride that she belonged to us,
The glamour she brought to many humdrum lives,
The daily round of comment and media fuss.

But now, the certain knowledge that
Like us, she made mistakes in life and love,
She will never grow old, our Queen of Hearts,
She died cocooned in happiness and love,
And our memories of her will never depart.

Pat Heppel

THE BURDEN OF INHERITANCE:
AROUND THE DEATH OF PRINCESS DIANA

It's not just oneself that one can affect
When marriages go wrong,
For others are hurt in ways indirect
And aftershocks are long.

No wonder she was confused.
Although of a name well-born,
Her earliest years were bruised,
By warring parents torn.

There wasn't a link of minds
When choice of a mate was made;
When glamorous fancy blinds,
A risky game is played.

As stage was then set to change,
The stupidest death burst in,
All counters to rearrange,
So thin is human skin.

By millions she was adored -
The national grief ran wild;
Some symbol had struck a chord,
As flower on flower was piled.

Let's pray that her brave young boys
Whose courage the nation saw
Don't learn how despair destroys,
But inspiration draw.

On magical island now
Beneath flowery carpet laid,
Their mother's own traits, somehow,
Perplexing, young, won't fade.

Anne Sanderson

MILLENNIUM MAN

A fearful screech drags sleep from the womb of night.
Like a fumbling robot he's washed and fed before it's light.
Then into a tin box on wheels to take him away,
To the same dull office for another boring day,
Making meaningless marks on paper that'll never matter
And drink cardboard coffee with iced chatter.

> I created everything you could want,
> Paradise fit for the highest angels,
> Animals, sun and seasons to share,
> Pleasures beyond your imagination.

At last it's five o'clock, a hooter pulls the chain,
That flushes him down the stair into his box again.
Crawls through polluted streets, slowly rolling back
Home to where the heart is, to where he can crack
A can and doze through TV to supper time or past.
Then to bed, another day gone - just like the last.

> I never dreamt it could go so wrong!
> Everything should be perfect in such
> A wonderful place, but even I, God
> Your creator, can make mistakes.

Mike Parker

GOD'S BLESSINGS

Everything is changing, as the days are going by,
Even the right to work, or flying through the sky.
The air is so polluted, and full of lead they say,
And even in our nation, we cannot pay our way.

Our roads are full of rubbish, the bins no longer full,
And everyone is hurrying, but children who walk to school.
The cost of everything we buy increases day by day
And yet the streets are lined with cars that never drive away.

But I know who never changes, our God remains the same,
He is always ready to listen to us when we pray through Jesus' name.
He created our world making us for himself
And will keep us from harm, maybe not with great wealth.

If you look around you will see wonderful things,
The snow in the winter, the warmth the sun brings.
The smile of a baby, the love of a friend,
The blessings God gives you, these never end.

Elsie Blackburn

DUNBLANE

Take a walk in the Scottish countryside.
To the people of Dunblane.
Feel the grief they must feel there.
Since the gunman went insane.

Imagine a mother and father.
With no child to kiss goodnight.
His toys still in his bedroom.
Unplayed with, but still in sight.

And all the children cry.
For the mates they will never see.
Their peace there lives in ribbons.
Oh God why should it be?

Jenny Bosworth

THE WONDER OF THIS WORLD

If I could write a story,
    Of this world and all its glory,
        A story of the beauty of creation.

The beauty of the flowers,
    The thunderstorms and showers,
        The beauty of each continent and nation.

I'd write of soaring mountains,
    Great glaciers, foaming fountains,
        Deep valleys, green and fertile, overflowing.

Rainforests, rolling hills,
    There would be no bitter pills,
        The world would be a garden, sweetly growing.

Where the streams and rivers tumble,
    As storm clouds gently rumble,
        Bringing purest water to the valleys.

Children would be singing,
    And church bells would be ringing,
        There'd be no hidden menace in dark alleys.

There'd be no pain and dying,
    No starving children crying,
        No guns or bombs to blow this world asunder.

So in my 'fairy story'
    We can dream of all this glory,
        And marvel at the world and all its wonder.

James W Sargant

REACHING FOR LIGHT

Seeing forced rhubarb on market shelf
I was transported way back in time
To a blacked-out shed-like building
Where Land Girls like me worked in line.

Each with candle on wrought iron stick
We moved a pace at a time
While pulling armfuls of rhubarb
Seen in circles of light combined.

And now, when mind tugs at memory
Like a dipping and dancing kite
I think of all those pretty pink stalks
Reaching up, ever hopeful of light.

Amelia Canning

KING HUSSAIN 1999

King Hussain
Died in pain

He had cancer
Let's find the answer

He was only 63
Oh dear me!

He was the King of Jordan
Of the Hashermite Kingdom.

There were thousands at his funeral
Ordinary people, politicians and royal

While Prince Abdullah was first behind the coffin
Then his brothers and politicians

Soldiers in green
           were to be seen

Keeping the crowd
           segregated from the procession
Thousands mourned and cried
As their King had died!

The procession of King Hussain
ended in *no pain!*

Marie Barker

D DAY 1944

The air was electric
Fraught with activity
Nobody speaking
Yet everyone knowing
It was about to happen.

Ships afloat waiting
They knew not what
With Nelsonic eye
One hurried past
As if they were not.

Of a sudden a whisper -
Prepare for action -
Day and night stand-by -
Torch, forms, help with survivors:
Pray God they'll not need us.

Came the dawn and a roaring
Planes droning on ever on:
Quiet the harbour now
Silent the mess,
Old sailors gathered with Wrens
Awaiting the news.

Sighs of relief at the landing - yet
But the start, in Churchillian phrase,
Of the great adventure.
Dunkirk in reverse.

Patricia Weitz

TITANIC

I was not yet born when the disaster happened
Nor did I see the great ship set sail,
But whenever I've heard or read of it since
Tears to my eyes never fail.
For such tragic and futile loss
Brought not about by a war
My imagination runs riot
striking to the core.

So many tales of courage, how brave
were those who could not be saved,
What must the Captain have suffered
Knowing his ship was so doomed?
Many disaster are natural events
Causing much loss, grief and pain,
But Titanic buried beneath the waves
Sails on in our hearts yet again.

Stories are told, films have been screened
most popular ever we hear;
Titanic holds such fascination
Since that fatal night it went down,
A fitting memorial to all the lost souls
Their memories live on in renown.

The great ship set sail
In all her splendour
There was expectation
As the voyage progressed, yet
No one expected an
Iceberg to strike - catastrophe
Chaos . . . cold . . . courage, curiosity . . .

Joan Heybourn

NEAR YET FAR!

Sometimes when I sit on my own,
I feel lonely and all alone.
But then I look at the sky so blue,
And know that same sky's over you.

The sun, the moon and the stars above,
There for all with God's heavenly love.
And though an ocean keeps us apart,
You're always there within my heart.

I think of technology and space,
The advancement of the human race.
And should I lift the phone I'd hear,
Your voice as tho' you were very near.

The world is not as large as it seems,
For I still see you in my dreams.
And though an ocean between us divides,
I know in your thoughts, you're by my side.

M Muirhead

NOVEMBER 22ND, 1963

Who could have guessed
That fateful day?
The shots rang out,
Blue skies turned grey.

Hard to believe
Story was true.
You remember?
So where were you?

At the bus stop
Standing so still.
Eerie silence,
An ice-cold chill.

Some assassin
Had lain in wait.
Chosen the place,
The time and date.

The car drew near
You aimed your gun.
Mayhem ensued,
The deed was done.

President dead
Was headline news.
So little gain,
So much to lose.

Aboard the bus
I went my way.
Changed forever
That fateful day.

Angela Pritchard

WHERE WAS I?

I placed a wreath upon the stone
Then, standing back I stood alone
In silence, and with thoughts profound,
I bowed my head, then looked around
To the place my crew had died,
As to the ground their aircraft dived.
But that was many years ago
When stationed here at Sullom Voe.
The drama of that winter's morn
Still in my mind so vivid borne!
But where was I that fateful day?
Standing in a ward not far away,
A witness to that ghastly scene,
And thinking now *what might have been!*

Reg Curwen

FATE

A seat by the fire is occupied by a man
With thoughts he hopes to hide
From my mother I heard this terrible tale
I listened and my face went pale

Through both World Wars he'd survived to tell
The first one for him a living hell

On the battlefields he'd fought that day
His injured and dying comrades lay
The rifle was shot from his hand
As he ran with that brave strong band

He turned as his mate fell dead
On the ground
Picked up his rifle, then swung around
He saw his Commander with pistol raised
A deserter he'd caught in the smoke-
Filled haze

He stopped just in time, my father was mine
On that terrible, terrible day

Poppy Ashfield

MILLENNIUM BUG

the hole in the wall doesn't dispense
the calculator doesn't tally
the stock market drops ten pence
while silicon melts in the valley

the washing machine doesn't clean
microwaves sustain a ping
video recorder flashes green
while the doorbell continues to ring

the traffic lights strobe primary
emergency services arrive late
the casualties cannot be treated
without a digital state

satellites shift in their course
oil tankers collide in the sea
people communicate by morse
resentful of technology

white flags in the trenches
mount ararat held the arc
we think we are so clever
because we can make a mark

B P S Weldon

A Hundred Years On . . .

Wither or wonder who we all are
A nation that breeds . . . continuously
No causing objections
No holding elections
No practising laws
Or submitting rules
No more inspecting and suspecting
Controlling and holding
A nation on guard
Come the next millennium
We will all learn to live
United we will give
A peaceful calm
And no given harm
United we will form
And never create a storm
With better communication
And a stable salvation
Our future will be
Mankind will be free . . .

Suzan Gumush

INFORMATION

We hope you have enjoyed reading this book - and that you will continue to enjoy it in the coming years.

If you like reading and writing poetry drop us a line, or give us a call, and we'll send you a free information pack.

Write to :-
Triumph House Information
Remus House
Coltsfoot Drive
Woodston
Peterborough
PE2 9JX
(01733) 898102